Russell Phillip Masters currently lives in Dorset. Paranormal sensitivity runs in his family and has been there for generations. Russell has been researching the paranormal from a young age, when he began experiencing the paranormal for himself. He now runs a team of 20 plus investigators, looking for hard evidence of the paranormal.

Best Wishes
New
HAPKC.

Dedication

This is dedicated to my children. May you have the courage to pursue all of your dreams, no matter how big or out of reach they may seem. Believe and you will achieve.

Love, Dad.

Russell Phillip Masters

So You Want to Be a Paranormal Investigator?

Austin Macauley Publishers™

LONDON · CAMBRIDGE · NEW YORK · SHARJAH

A CIP catalogue record for this title is available from the British Library.

ISBN 9781787107182 (Paperback)
ISBN 9781787106888 (E-Book)

www.austinmacauley.com

First Published (2018)
Austin Macauley Publishers Ltd™
25 Canada Square
Canary Wharf
London
E14 5LQ

Acknowledgements

Thank you to *www.paranormaldatabase.com* for allowing me to use your website for reference.

Thank you to all of my team: John, Chris, Dave, Josh, Amber, Holly, Ross, Mum, Ben, Karina, Lisa, Jemma, Sally, Rob, Allan, Tracy, Donna, Kieran, Jack, Paula, my guides, my grandparents and our ancestry. Thanks to everyone at Austin Macauley for publishing and believing in this book.

Contents

Foreword

I have been interested in the paranormal from a young age. I saw, felt and heard things that I did not understand. My mum experienced the same, as did my grandfather and other relatives. We were brought up to respect nature and the magic within it. The gift of paranormal sensitivity runs in both sides of my family. My mum was taught to read tea leaves at the age of ten and she recalls her nan using bowls of water for divination. My mum still reads the tarot, crystal ball and tea leaves now. However, she only does this for friends and family free of charge as she does not believe in charging for the gifts she was given or inherited. So if any trolls are reading this, you are going to need a new angle, good luck.

Coming from this kind of background, you would be right to assume that I am either deluded or my investigations are biased and the evidence I have recorded up to now has been the result of group hysteria. But you would be wrong. I like to be tested. The whole reason I still investigate the paranormal is that I am aware of what I see, hear and feel. I don't need any one to clarify this for me. I earn no money from my investigations, so money is not an incentive.

I want hard evidence. You will always have non-believers and sceptics and I invite sceptics on investigations with my team as they give a non-biased reasoning to an investigation.

When you have seen something as much as myself and my team, it is easy to get swept up into the hysteria of the paranormal. In fact, a few of the newer members of my team were sceptics until they came on an investigation. My team and I use all the latest theories associated with the paranormal and all the latest scientific technology to aid us in our investigation. We also debunk more than we record but still have a vast array of evidence on file that could not be debunked.

This book has been written for those with an interest in paranormal investigation and will help you stay safe if you choose to begin investigating.

Happy Hunting.
Stay Blessed.

Evidence for the Paranormal

Ghosts, spirits and paranormal activity have been reported since the beginning of recorded history, all over the world. It used to be estimated that one in ten people would see a ghost in their life time. I estimate that that statistic is now highly outdated. And it is my belief that this is down to society. It seems the more we learn about genetics and the human body and the mind, the more we are opening up our senses. More people than ever are now meditating and eating healthier and more people are taught to share feelings and experiences to prevent illness and disease. It is for these reasons listed that I would say that seven in ten people will see a ghost spirit or experience the paranormal in their lifetimes.

Ghosts, How Do You See Them?

This is usually the first question I am asked by people joining us on our investigations. And I will give you the same advice that I give them.

Stay open minded, take lots of pictures, have a good time and don't get swept up in the excitement. Stay level-headed and keep an investigative mind. Another thing is trust what you are feeling, hearing, smelling and tasting. You may have an internal monologue present in your mind; listen to it as this is how spirits/ ghosts and your spirit guides may try and communicate so as not to scare you. If you do listen to the monologue, ask if the message comes in love.

Anything that means you harm at this point will leave as they will assume you are experienced in the paranormal. They won't waste their time with you when they can influence weak timid people.

If you feel the need to keep looking in a certain area on the investigation or feel you are being watched, this is a good time to take some pictures. Or if you feel cold, dizzy or sick, call a member of your team over and ask them to take some pictures of you. In my experience, it is these feelings that provide the most evidence for and against the paranormal as the feelings above can also be the results of EMF. I will explain EMF fields in more detail later in this book. But for now, I will leave it there. Remember many things that at first appear paranormal, may not actually be such.

If you feel that you are already sensitive to the paranormal, you will need to train it through meditation, or join a circle. There are many circles out there that specialise in training people to control and improve these gifts. And they will ensure you are safe throughout. You will also be taught how to recognise entities, control and dismiss entities and unwanted spirits/ ghosts etc.

Blessings

Before your investigation begins, if you have paid to join an investigation at one of the many venues offering investigations such as fright nights, you will be asked to join in on a blessing before you begin. Some blessings may be religious or prayers. If you do not have a religion or have a strong religion, do not be put off by this, it is designed to keep you and your group safe and your guide will ask whoever they pray to for protection.

I myself have many friends of different religions and from different backgrounds and I am aware of this when I am leading an investigation. Therefore, when I do a blessing, I make no reference to a higher being. My team and I will stand in a circle and hold hands and I will lead them in a guided meditation, where I ask them to close their eyes and imagine a light source emulating from their bodies and together, we move this light source all over are bodies and we pass it around to others in our group. I do it this way as not to disrespect anyone's beliefs and so far, touch wood, I have kept myself and my group safe using this method.

Different Types of Hauntings

A haunting is described by the psychic library 2011 as a paranormal phenomenon where spirits or supernatural beings materialise or an historical event is seen as if it is happening all over again. (*http://psychiclibrary.com/2011*)

There are considered to be around five different types of hauntings that have been recorded throughout the ages.

The First Is a Residual Haunting:

A residual haunting is said to occur when a traumatic or stressful event such as a rape or murder has taken place in a certain location. Negative energy is bouncing around the atmosphere and it causes the event to continue to play over and over again. Some paranormal theorists suggest that the stone stores the event and bounces the memory of the event around the location. So you see the event as if you were watching the television. There is no interaction with this type of haunting as it is just the memory of the event. Much evidence of this type of haunting has been recorded from hotels to battlefields.

Poltergeist Activity

This is the most well-known type of haunting, thanks to TV/film and media. Poltergeist literally means noisy ghost. In the films, poltergeist activity is described as an angry spirit that moves stuff, breaks and hides stuff and sometimes causes physical harm. Poltergeists can be mischievous or violent. Some cases reported support the theory that poltergeist activity can be the result of angry spirits who are trying to interact and feel ignored. However, much of the modern-day research that has been carried out on poltergeist activity suggests that poltergeist activity could be in fact the result of Psychokinesis. Psychokinesis is often recorded under its abbreviated name PK.

Psychokinesis is the ability to move things using the mind. In most recorded cases involving poltergeist activity, one common denominator was found to be consistent in all cases. The home that reported the activity had a teenager living in it who was going through puberty. The majority of evidence gave reference to a female teenager but some cases involved males. It was found that the poltergeist activity reported could have been the result of a teenager using PK energy subconsciously in response to changes within the body, stress and anger, feelings we all went through during puberty.

Parapsychologists will continue to investigate this phenomenon. I would not rule out angry spirits completely though. I remember when our house was repossessed, we were housed in what was called a halfway home that was built in the 18th century. We had to make more room, so we knocked down a false wall.

Behind the wall was an old cooker with burn marks up the wall and on the floor and burnt kid's toys. And from that day on, I was hearing and seeing stuff again. I attempted to ignore what I heard and shut it off. For months after, I remember my door was fitted with a yell lock, which was always left on the catch. When we knocked the false wall down, the door would lock on its own and my stereo would turn on as loud as it would go, I slept through it but my parents are light sleepers and they knew what was going on as both are sensitive, but they agreed not to tell me to protect me and not put me off using my gift in the future.

It came to a head one night when I needed the toilet. I opened the door and began to walk down the long corridor towards the toilet, the light bulb shot out of the ceiling, rose, smashing in front of me. I felt something begin to run at me and I ran into my parents' bedroom. The morning after, my parents became concerned for my and my sister's safety. They moved all our stuff into their room and we all shared one bedroom until we were rehoused. I had just turned 13, so this could have been PK energy, but I am still convinced this was a result of ignoring the spirit trying to talk to me. But I guess I will never know as they knocked the house down shortly after we moved.

Demons

I have been lucky enough to not ever encounter a demon that I am aware of, so this is based purely on texts and scriptures that I have read.

Demons are entities that have never had mortal or human form.

They are entities of pure energy. They are manipulative and apparently can take any form. Their main goal is to break down a person's free will, with the intention of taking over the body. Demons are said to be able to attach themselves to people as well as objects and also appear as dark mists, clouds etc. If you encounter a demon, the first thing you sense will more than likely be the smell of sulphur. Unfortunately, there is nothing more I can tell you about demons except if you think the haunting is due to a demon energy, you will need to seek a demonologist or an exorcist.

Demons have been written about since the first written history records so maybe there is such a thing as demons. Like any spirit, they can only enter if you allow them to. The method I have been taught is to ask if a spirit comes in love. This is usually enough to deter them as they will not waste their time on someone who shows no fear as demons prey on the weak or people who invite them in. One of the most common ways of inviting demons and other dark entities in is by way of the Ouija board. Something I did experience on an investigation with fright nights was the smell of sulphur. I told the medium leading the investigation, who had also studied demonology. He said the smell of sulphur has been associated with demon energy for years and led us away from the location for safety. So, if you smell sulphur, please do not take any chances and move to a different area, unless you are lucky enough to be with a demonologist.

Intelligent Hauntings

Einstein's theory suggests that we are all energy beings on a quantum level. We are made of atoms and neutrons and electrical impulses. Therefore, when we die, the energy that powers our mortal vessel leaves, carrying with it memories of what we used to be and what we knew and what we felt. Therefore, in theory, we should be able to still communicate with beings of the mortal realm, regardless of a lack of body.

Intelligent hauntings are probably the most common hauntings as most of the evidence recorded for the paranormal consists of EVP in response to questions asked when investigating the paranormal. It is said that the spirit realm operates on a different frequency to our own and therefore, we may not be able to hear them talking directly to us.

Other responses recorded are investigators asking for signs of a spiritual presence, for example, many paranormal investigators would say something like: if you are here, throw something, move the glass, move the table etc. This is called 'calling out' and there are many reports and even video evidence that show clear responses from unseen energies to an investigator calling out. I agree that some of this video evidence may have been created for entertainment value, so is not considered 100% proof of the paranormal.

Shadow People

This kind of haunting has no real explanation. They are dark, shapeless figures that are seen usually through the peripheral vision. They have been recorded walking through walls, they tend not to wear any clothing; however, this is contradicted by a number of sightings of shadow people wearing hoods and robes. Shadow people are described by clairvoyants and sensitive as non-human entities.

They do not communicate; they sometimes are seen as smoke or steam. My personal feeling is that shadow people are no different from residual entities, just echoes of a time past, stored in stone. Shadow creatures and animals have also been recorded but again, I believe that they are just echoes of times past.

Your First Investigation

What do you need?

Here it is:

You have a rough idea of where you are going to go, you have watched every episode of most haunted and ghost hunters for the past three weeks.

What do you need?

*Warm clothing
*A torch
*A flask
*A camera, preferably digital
*A notepad and pen
Also, it is a good idea to take loads of spare batteries.

Another item that can be useful and purchased cheaply is a dictaphone. You can also download a dictaphone to your phone. That is all you will need for your first investigation. If you are going on a paid investigation with a company such as Fright Nights, you will be introduced to various items used by paranormal investigators and will have a chance to try them out for yourself. However, if you are going alone or with a friend, you will only need the bare essentials mentioned above.

Investigating Successfully Using Basic Equipment

First things first.

Remember your blessing before you start. You can google blessings or simply pray for protection from whoever or whatever you believe in.

After your blessing, you are ready to begin.

The first paid investigation I went on was to a fort in Essex. The magnitude of the fort and the setting was enough to ignite the imagination. But I remained level-headed and sceptical. I lost count of the number of people I saw pouring salt around their car and I knew they had already lost to their imagination and emotions. The problem with this on an investigation is that all evidence becomes paranormal, with no room for the science of paranormal investigation, causing you to spiral into hysteria, leaving you with loose evidence of the paranormal at most.

My advice to you: enjoy yourself, take loads of pictures, listen to your instincts and inner voice, but remain in an investigative frame of mind and do not let your emotions or imagination carry you into a frenzy. Hopefully, after your investigation, you will have a lot of evidence to go through and debunk. All that cannot be debunked may be recorded as evidence of the paranormal and submitted if you like or kept for your records. This is up to you.

Be aware, if you have now got the proverbial bug for the paranormal, it is quite common to start looking on eBay for other equipment to aid your future investigations. This is fine as the more equipment you have, the more thorough your investigation will be. However, just a word of advice: do not buy everything straight away as there are a lot of sites that rip off the paranormal investigator. Many items can be purchased cheaply if you know what you are looking for.

I now make most of the equipment myself using YouTube for reference. One of the best sites for this is Viper Paranormal, where there are many videos on how to make your own equipment for around £5.00.

What Is in My Kit?

I do not carry a lot of equipment as many investigations involve lots of walking around and if you are carrying a lot of kit, you may miss vital evidence.

My Kit

Digital Camera

A digital camera can be purchased for about three to five pounds now. I have adapted mine to work as a full spectrum camera, a modification I completed in about ten minutes. There are many videos on YouTube that will walk you through the modification process. Basically, a full spectrum camera allows you to see a full spectrum of colours not visible to the human eye. Evidence suggests that the spirit realm runs parallel with our own but the human eye restricts us from seeing the full spectrum of colours. However, for the camera to view the full spectrum of colour, all you do is remove the IR filter from the camera lens, allowing you to take pictures of a full spectrum of colour. You will know this has worked when you take a picture and the picture appears pink or purple in colour like the pictures overleaf.

Infrared Thermometer Gun

The next item I have in my kit is an infrared thermometer gun.

An infrared thermometer gun is a tool used by air condoning technicians and plumbers to locate leaks and blockages. Much recorded evidence of the paranormal report unexplained temperature changes before coming into contact with spirits, ghosts or entities. It is for this reason that we use infrared thermometers to locate temperature changes that may produce evidence of the paranormal.

It is vital in an investigation to rule out all other reasons for temperature changes, such as windows, doors, drains, holes in mortar and air vents. If there is no logical reason for temperature changes, you may record your findings as possible paranormal activity.

You can pick up infrared thermometers in most DIY shops for around £6.00 to £45.00. However, from a so called paranormal investigation shop you could pay anything from £60.00-£120.00.

I understand everyone has to make a living, however, most of the owners of these shops have never investigated the paranormal in their life and have simply seen a gap in the market to make easy money.

Wire Detector used by Electricians.

The next piece of equipment in my kit is a wire detector used by electricians to find hidden wires and power sources that are hidden behind walls. As well as locating hidden electrical sources, a wire detector can be used to locate changes in electromagnetic frequencies. A popular belief held by paranormal researchers is that ghosts, spirits or entities emit their own electromagnetic frequency thus causing a disturbance in the natural EMF found all around us.

Although much modern research is steering away from this theory due to the many variables that can affect EMF fields such as man-made power sources like mobile phones, plug sockets, railway lines to name a few. I however use the wire detector to debunk paranormal activity. It has been proven, tried and tested that with enough man-made electronics in one area, a person nearby can start to feel sick, dizzy, paranoid and even hallucinate; these are also the symptoms that have been recorded by people who have experienced paranormal events in the past. So as an investigator, it is going to be your job to rule out man-made EMF fields before you start an investigation.

Dictaphones

A Dictaphone should be one of the first items you buy for your kit.

You can purchase one like mine above or there are also many Dictaphone apps that can be downloaded to your phone.

It is believed that the spirit realm operates on a higher frequency to our own, so unless gifted or trained, you will be unable to communicate directly with a spirit. However, EVP or electronic voice phenomena is usually found when you get home and plug your phone or Dictaphone into the computer as you can enhance the sound of your audio clip. EVP is often a recorded response in the form of an answer to a question you ask of the entity, spirit, or ghost. We call this line of questioning calling out. Typical questions but not conclusive are open ended question such as "Did you die here?", "Do you need help?" "Are you happy?" and "We are here?" etc., etc. You get the picture.

Another item I have in my collection is known as a spirit box. A spirit box is a device that uses white noise. It works by quickly scanning AM and FM radio waves producing white noise. Spirits, entities and ghosts are said to use the white noise from the spirit box to form words. A spirit box is more effective if you combine your Dictaphone and the spirit box together. A lot of the most recent evidence has been recorded using this combination of equipment. But do not waste a lot of money purchasing a spirit box as you can make one from around £3.99 to £5.99. Later, I will tell you how to make one in eight simple steps.

How to Make a Spirit Box

Step One: Go to your local supermarket store that sells leisure items as well as groceries. Head up the escalator or head to the leisure area.

Step Two: Select a battery operated AM/ FM radio priced from £3.99-£5.99. Take it to the check out.

Step Three: Exchange goods for cash or use your debit card, it is completely up to you.

Step Four: Get it home but if you can't wait get into the car.

Step Five: Remove packaging.

Step Six: Insert batteries.

Step Seven: Unscrew or snap off aerial attached.

Step Eight: Turn on.

There you have it. A fully functioning spirit box that does not cost the earth. Here is mine.

There are many more tools for paranormal investigators but remember you may have to carry it around with you. If you do a bit of research, most tools can be made or purchased cheaply, as all the tools were originally designed for another purpose but adapted to investigate the paranormal. Type in to YouTube, 'make your own ghost hunting equipment' and thousands of videos will come up. There is no need to pay the earth.

Terminology and Debunking

Orbs = What Exactly Is an Orb?

An orb is an anomaly often discovered in pictures. It presents as a random ball of light that varies in colour. Some even appear to have facial features when blown up. No one knows exactly what these balls of light are; however, a popular belief is that they are the spirit energy we all possess that is trapped inside our mortal vessel. Some understand this as chi or a life source. But until we are freed from are mortal vessels, we will never be sure.

Some orbs can be debunked. Insects flying in direct light of a camera could present as an orb or reflections from mirrors can present as an orb. The pictures I have of orbs however, are extremely bright in colour and when I see an orb I go through a sequence of debunking. I clean the lens of the camera and take the picture in exactly the same way. I list possible causes such as mirrors etc. I make sure I record the time and the colour.

This is a picture of my mum at a family BBQ. I took the first picture when I saw the orb on her lower arm; I then went through my debunking process. I cleaned the lens, asked her to move and retook the picture. The orb was still there. I changed my position and the orb was still there. I looked at the position of the glass blown up to see if the orb could be the result of the sun shining through the glass. The glass was not positioned in a way that reflected the sun at the angle it presented on my mother's body. I took this picture using my Nikon d3300 DSLR camera.

Electromagnetic Field or EMF

Electromagnetic fields are all around us. Natural fields and man-made fields.

An EMF reader detects disturbances in the electromagnetic fields. Spirits, ghosts and entities are also made up of electromagnetic energy and therefore when they are around, it is believed that they interrupt the fields in our realm. An EMF reader detects this disturbance and can lead to a good collection of evidence for the paranormal. One of the problems with EMF fields and the paranormal is the symptoms of coming into contact with spirit and into contact with EMF Fields; the feelings recorded mimic each other. Sickness, dizziness, feelings of paranoia and unease and temperature changes in the body are all common when coming into contact with either as they are both made up of the same energy.

An easy way of debunking paranormal from EMF is observation.

1: Arrive to the investigation location early, so you can have a good look around and take notes of areas that may have high EMF levels. Look for pylons, overloaded plug sockets and other areas where there are a lot of electrical appliances.

2: Use your EMF reader or a map reading compass.

Using the compass, you find true north and head towards it. If the compass pin turns more than 45 degrees, you are looking at an EMF field.

3: If you find yourself within a strong EMF field, only picture evidence will count as solid evidence so start snapping pictures.

Mediums/Psychics/Sensitives /Clairvoyant

A medium is someone who communicates with spirit. Everyone has the power to communicate with the spirit realm but many factors are said to influence these abilities for better or for worse.

One of the latest theories is that chloride in water and tooth paste dulls the senses causing a layer of callus to form over the pineal gland which is said to be the part of the brain that allows us to communicate with a spirit. This is also known as the third eye or pineal body. I advise every one of my team to drink mineral water as opposed to tap water a week before an investigation and leading up to the investigation and many of my team mates are noticing a difference in the evidence they are gathering. I can't say if this theory is true as I cannot open someone's brain and see it working 24 hours a day but the evidence being gathered is a lot more frequent.

Clairvoyance is the ability to see and communicate with spirits and other entities.

A sensitive: A sensitive is what I class myself as. It is the ability of extreme empathy that allows the sensitive to feel the emotions of the entities/spirits/ghosts that have passed over. It is these feelings that allow the sensitive to connect with the spirit realm.

These abilities I possess (excuse the pun) also work with the living. When working as a mental health support worker on the psychiatric intensive care ward, I noticed many people were afraid to say too much; even the staff were afraid to talk too much. I would not have mentioned my abilities or my family's abilities to anyone in the hospital. The senior staff often wondered how I knew the things I knew about the patients when they were admitted to the ward and how I could build rapport so quickly with the patients. It was down to being a sensitive. I could feel what they were feeling and what they were trying to say when they could not get their words to work in sentences, thanks to the negative symptoms of schizophrenia and mania. This is also how I communicate with spirit.

Psychics can predict people's future, but this term has become a "pigeon hole term" for most people in touch with the spirit realm. Some psychics can communicate and are given glimpses of people's futures by receiving messages from the spirit realm.

Entity: An entity is something that is considered not of human origin from the spirit realm. Entities are recorded as tricksters, poltergeist, and demons etc.

Spirit: A spirit that is believed to be the energy source that was once trapped inside a human body that now has become free from its mortal vessel.

Residual Haunting: A residual haunting is a like a memory of past. These kinds of hauntings usually involve no communication. In fact, they do not even acknowledge you are there. This is probably the most common of hauntings.

EMF Pump: A handmade device that creates an electromagnetic field. The EMF is now concentrated to one area allowing a spirit to use a concentrated magnetic field to manifest. Once again, paranormal retailers will charge you a fortune for one of these but if you YouTube EMF pumps, there are many detailed videos on how to make your own for about £6.00.

EVP: Electronic voice phenomenon. These are sounds found on voice recordings or video recordings which are considered to be the voice of a disembodied spirit. These can be enhanced by combining a spirit box and a Dictaphone or voice recorder on your phone.

Most investigators using the above combination will ask questions of the spirits. The idea being, the spirits can then use the FM/AM radio scanning for words they can use to answer the question.

There is much more terminology that paranormal investigators use. However, this will get you through the majority of investigations.

Investigations and evidence
Collected by everything supernatural
September 2015
Time: 23: 30
Location: Church Knowles
BH21 5AE Camborne Dorset
History: Built in the 12th century on a Neolithic ritual site.
Arrived at Knowlton Church at approx.: 23.30.
Parking was restricted.
Note: Car share for future investigations.
Stats:
4 gifted
4 sceptics
4 new investigators
4 experienced – one plus years
Base EMF Reading: Moderate
Vision: No lighting, natural or artificial.

We arrived at Knowlton Church at approx. 23:30. This was a relatively big investigation; 18 of us showed up.

This was the second time I had been to Knowlton Church. The pictures of ruins lay in the back of a full moon, and you could feel the excitement building amongst all the investigators. The full moon shining on the ruins made the setting extremely atmospheric.

Upon entering the farm-style gate, I was informed by my guides that we would be welcomed and protected throughout the investigation as I would be amongst my own people. This was confirmed when we arrived at the outer ring of Knowlton Church. The feeling of belonging and protection was extremely comforting. I saw the Neolithic people in my mind's eye holding hands around the outer ring. This was the perfect location for the blessing. The blessing always makes me nervous as it is impossible to judge how new people joining the team will respond when you tell them to form a circle, hold hands and close their eyes. Unfortunately, it is the only way I know how to protect my team from negative entities.

Once the blessing was over, it was time to introduce the equipment we would be using on this investigation and explain the concept of hysteria, so people would not let their imaginations get the better of them.

Once everyone was briefed I placed the Dictaphone in the ruins of the church and everyone branched off into groups. The church ruins were made from stone and slate. In its day, this church would have looked amazing, as it stands in the middle of open space, with nothing else around it except a small wooded area.

See pictures over leaf. I have included some pictures with orbs in them and others that we believe to be good evidence for the paranormal. The pink/purple grain photos were taken via full spectrum while the others were taken using a normal digital camera.

We began the investigation and left the Dictaphone recording inside the church. The first paranormal contact came quickly and I was called over by one of my team, Kris. Kris is one of the naturally gifted members of the team. He had felt a presence inside the ruins and wanted me to check it out. John, another naturally gifted psychic and I rounded up the rest of the team and we entered the ruins.

We took a base line reading from the infrared thermometer gun and the EMF detector we would attempt to initiate a response form whatever or whoever it was. I began calling out in attempt to establish contact. I felt that the presence was there; however, whatever it was, was doing its best to evade us. We needed another angle. As my current line of calling out was not working. It was decided that we should try to illicit an emotional response from whatever it was. Now, before I go any further I do not recommend this line of questioning to the beginner unless you have someone of experience with you. The church was built on a Neolithic site and a place of worship for the Neolithic people. The church was built to invalidate the Neolithic people's beliefs and force their own beliefs onto them. So this is where I started.

"I cannot believe you class yourself as holy men. Really hiding in shadows like rats. Is that how you overcame the Neolithic people?"

"Hiding like rats until they were sleeping."

Log: No Response

"Do you think or maybe that's why you are stuck here? Your own god does not want you."

Log: Dictaphone fell from the ruins onto the floor.

Kris: Continued this line of questioning whilst I checked out the Dictaphone and the wall it fell from.

Kris: "Do you not want us here?"

"How do you think the settlers here felt when you built your church?"

It was at this point that three to four of us heard music playing in the distance.

Log: check local entertainment guides that may have been happening locally to Knowlton Church.

I could find no reason for the Dictaphone falling. There was no wind. The part on which Dictaphone was originally lying on was a flat surface, which was the reason we placed the Dictaphone there in the first place. Also inside the ruins some walls still provided shelter from external elements.

Kris and John decided to carry on with the same line of questioning as it appeared to be producing the responses we were looking for.

Just then, I was called to an external part of the ruins, a wooded area approximately ten to fifteen foot away from the ruins of church. I was met by four other members of my team who reported they heard something run into the wooded area. I explained that in this environment, it could be a hedgehog, a fox or rat or other wild life.

I made my way into the wooded area. It was extremely dark. I took my torch out and turned it on. Illuminated by torch light were ribbons of many different colours tied to branches. It was amazing as each of the ribbons had wishes attached, greetings, messages of hope and peace. It was beautiful. I snapped a few full spectrum pictures in the wooded area.

In this wooded area, I felt a strong sense of belonging and peace. Just then I sensed a presence. Her name was Rebecca in my mind's eye and I could see she was about 24–25 years old. I sensed that her body or vessel was destroyed by cancer. She was so familiar to me although we had never met; it felt like we had known each other. I was then joined by the four investigators who were waiting outside the wooded area who had heard me talking and approached with caution in case I had lost the plot.

There was no need to ask if Rebecca came in love. The love was radiating out of her. I asked if she knew about the church and the site. She told me the wooded area we stood in was known as the wishing tree or kissing tree. I was losing the connection but before she left, I promised to take her a pink ribbon and tie it to the tree the next time I visited and I plan to do this the next time I visit. I have included a picture of the site. But you have to see it for yourself as the photo does not do it justice and I cannot believe I never saw this first time I visited Knowlton Church. Continuing the investigation, we headed back to Kris, John and the others in the ruins of the church. As I approached the doorway of the ruins, I sensed a hand on my throat and fell back just a couple of steps out of the ruins doorway.

"What was that?" "Is that all you have got?" I made my way back through the door Kris and John reported that they saw something move and followed it. In this part of the ruin, there was a hole where the window used to be. I took an EMF reading and one of the others took various temperature readings. The temperature read considerably lower in the window, a common occurrence. No glass exposure to the elements. (Log: debunked occurrence) Pictures full spectrum and a couple of digital shots. To debunk further. Looking through the window.

(Log: lights from passing cars could present as orbs or cause shadows to form. Road thirty to forty feet away from ruins. Still possible pseudo signs of the paranormal.) Action: review evidence when at home.

The investigation carried on for a further 30 minutes. Before we cleared away the stuff and headed back to the car it was now 0300 hours. We said our good byes and left.

The day after, it was time to start processing the evidence acquired. I started by uploading the pictures taken and requested the pictures taken by the other Investigators. They were sent to me to start trailing through. I put in my headphones and began listening to the EVP recordings on my Dictaphone whilst looking at the pictures.

There were many points of interest we captured on the Dictaphone. One compelling piece of evidence was the music heard. I then checked local events that may have been responsible but at that time of night there was none. I would almost definitely class Knowlton Church as one of the most active sites I have investigated and would recommend it to anyone.

I could brag on about the many investigations we have lead; however, I just wanted to give you a look at a typical investigation so you know what to expect.

Pictures Taken of Knowlton Church Investigation Carried out by Everything Supernatural

Some of the pictures below have been singled out from these pictures in case you did not see the apparitions and orbs present.

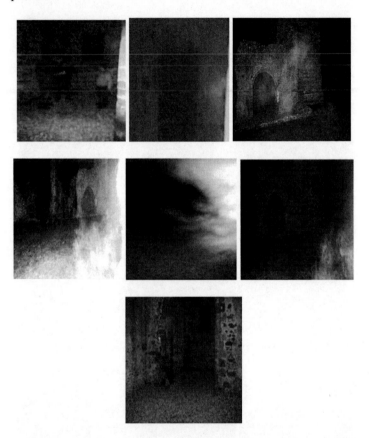

This is the same window as the picture above but taken with full spectrum. The reason we took the picture with a digital camera was that the orb had been witnessed seconds before the other picture was taken. I will not say what I saw in the picture above so as not to influence you or your thoughts in any way, as suggestion can also act as a factor in hysteria. But everyone who has seen this particular picture confirms what it is I see. To me, this is one of the best pictures taken and it was not even taken using a full spectrum camera.

Where to Investigate

Every town, village, city, county and country have their own myths, legends and ghost stories.

Something I have learned over the years; there is usually no smoke without fire. Although some stories evolve as the years go by usually by the Chinese whispers method, these stories are still worth checking out as the stories had to start somewhere.

Something I have experienced of late though in relation to investigations is a lot of places are refusing investigations to take place at the venues they manage. Some have religious reasons for this and I respect their beliefs and do not push the matter once they have refused. Others report that they have had mediums and priests etc. coming in to bless their venues to good effect. They therefore, do not want to increase the activity once it has been subdued and again I respect their reasoning for refusing investigations. However, some places that obviously are in desperate need of any source of income and who are advertising their venue as being haunted try and gain custom yet they are unwilling for their venues to be investigated which could increase their custom if a haunting is proved.

So venues are extremely hard to find without a lot of research. However, if you stick to what you know this will help.

Churches and Graveyards

Possibility of seeing anything is quite limited in my opinion. As once freed from the mortal vessel, why would you hang around your rotting corpse? As an analogy, when you scrap a car do you visit it in the scrap yard? Probably not.

However, feelings will play a big part in your decision on where to investigate. If you have a feeling when you walk past somewhere, it is worth researching this area.

A friend of mine, part of 'The Everything Supernatural Team', Kris was walking past a grave yard in a small seaside town of Portland and was feeling drawn to the site. He has since booked us an investigation there. And we are investigating in the beginning of October with the chance of doing a lock in the near future as the doors automatically lock at 1900 hours and will not unlock until 0700.

We have researched the site and there have been murderers, victims of murders etc. laid to rest there. All the ingredients for a successful investigation.

Castles and other Historical Sites

These are among the best places to investigate and where the most evidence has been collected. This may be due to overactive imaginations or the fact that most historical texts are recorded as a result of conflict. During conflict many emotions are present and unfortunately many people died protecting these sites. These places could be Neolithic, Roman, used in warfare, sites of murders and sites of ambushes to name a few.

Houses

These are probably the hardest to investigate. So many factors mentioned in earlier chapters play a factor. Such as teenagers living there. As I explained, research suggests that teenagers going through puberty may be responsible for events that seem paranormal but maybe it's a result of PK, an abbreviation of psychokinesis. Young children usually under ten years old are a good indication of house hauntings.

It is my belief that the reason for this is the more information we take in we have to shut down certain areas of the brain to accommodate the new information being absorbed and I believe this is when we shut off the psychic abilities, the brain is capable of performing. Unfortunately, some will never rediscover these abilities.

I believe that due to my dyslexia, this is why I am still in touch with these abilities. I believe that if research was carried out on people with psychic abilities, there would be a significant number of psychics/mediums etc. that would have been diagnosed as dyslexic. Unfortunately, at present, I do not possess the income to carry out research in this area but with what I know about the mind, brain and emotions, I am almost convinced of this link.

Another link I have noticed is the majority of the people interested in paranormal investigation work in law enforcement, security and nursing so maybe, the amount of empathy these jobs require attributes to such behaviour. Maybe what we now call empathy is in fact related to the psychic area of the brain.

Museums

Museums are great places to investigate. As they are full of historical items that will more than likely hold some personal significance to someone. John Zaffis known to some as the haunted collector star of the American TV series of the same name has over 40 years' experience in paranormal investigation and his investigations have provided evidence that sometimes spirits ghosts or entities can become attached to items of personal significance.

Having never met John Zaffis, I do not understand his evidence fully and I am limited in what I have read and watched of the haunted collector. But to me, this makes perfect sense. If you think of everyday items that you possess, use or wear that on the surface would appear invaluable, maybe even tatty to some, but to you they are a proverbial spiritual blanket, that if you lost, you would be devastated. Then why would you not need that same spiritual blanket in the afterlife?

Other evidence recorded supports this theory also and there have been many reports from mediums that in order for them to assist in crossing someone over they have had to ensure that a particular item the spirit was attached to be returned to a resting place of their choice. This may explain the need for leaving heirlooms. Maybe this then in turn acts as a spiritual anchor that allows the spirit to be close and watch over their loved ones and in turn, provide comfort for loved ones. This is the positive version so therefore, for every positive a negative must exist and from what I know of John Zaffis, this is where his particular expertise would come in. An example I can think of off of the top of my head is the Annabelle doll that currently resides in John Zaffis museum: a place I plan to visit one day.

Consider adding herbs and spices to your kit list

For thousands of years, herbs and spices have been used in the protection against paranormal forces. Again, we have to be careful here not to lose sight of your main goal, which is to investigate the paranormal and collect and record evidence. However, an investigation in my opinion must investigate all areas of the paranormal. So, I have chosen to include this section to enhance your knowledge and provide you with other things to help enhance your investigations.

The first herb I will mention is named Agrimony, which grows throughout most of Europe in woodland and fields, but it can also be cultivated at home.

Agrimony is said to banish evil spirits and deflect hostile magic by carrying it with you. Another myth of agrimony is that if placed under the pillow of sleeping person they will remain in a deep sleep until it is removed.

The second plant is a Dandelion,

Dandelions are said to enhance psychic ability by adding the powdered root, dried flowers or leaves to a smoking blend or placing them in a tea. If you choose to do this, please research the correct amounts etc. as I am not a plant expert or herbalist and have not used this method myself.

Images were taken by the author, Russell Phillips.

The third is a mallow

Often assumed to be a weed, it grows everywhere and is said to attract benevolent spirits and also helps in grounding them to the realm aiding better communication between the spirits and ourselves. Mallow is often white in colour.

Mallow is also said to be used to prevent possession. It is also considered an exorcism herb that can be used by a professional exorcist to rid a person of the entity or spirit that has taken over a person.

It is said that the best way to use mallow is to make a cold infusion steeped over night with the fresh roots. Or you can use the leaves to make an ointment.

The fourth is the poplar bud or pine bud.

Poplar buds have been used for years but the smell is somewhat of a required taste. When dried, burned and ground, they make a very good replacement for sage, which can be used for smudging, purification and for blessings. Smudging is an age-old technique that has been used worldwide for centuries, to rid an area of negativity, or protect against evil forces.

The poplar buds should be dried and tied together. Placed into a clay bowl and set alight. The smoke is then spread around the area you want to cleanse. If you google smudging you will get a more in-depth guide on smudging. I have used smudging on a few investigations sometimes before, sometimes after.

The fifth herb is Rowen.

Once again, rowen has been used for hundreds maybe thousands of years in magical practices and in rituals. Rowen is said to add power to any magical spell/ritual. For us though its uses include protection from possession, and spirits. It is said in folklore that a woman stood near a grave with a rowen staff and summoned the spirit to her and when the spirit arrived, she compelled it to tell her the truth. Once satisfied the spirit had not lied, she compelled the spirit back to the grave. If you have the skills you can make a rowen wand, bracelet or necklace for the investigation and test the theory.

The last herb I will recommend is St John's wort

This is the plant for the untrained psychic/medium or sensitive. Although St John's Wort has many medicinal properties, it is said to have many paranormal properties.

It can be placed in a silk bag or tied into a scarf it can then be hung above the door of your home or on the rear-view mirror of the car you take to your investigation to stop spirits and entities following you home. It can also be used to make holy water.

Recipe for holy water.
Use a jar, add spring water salt and St John's wort. You then have your own holy water.

How to use Holy Water for Cleansing or Possession

Take your home made holy water around the house with you and place your fingers in the concoction and flick the holy water off the end of your fingers shouting: 'Valente's'.

Again, there are many more plants/herbs that can be used for the paranormal. But let's start off at a basic level as investigators we should test our predecessor's theories as well as the theories of new researchers, enhancing our investigations.

Another area we as investigators should give precedence to is the use of crystals, gems and minerals. Once again, these have been used for hundreds maybe thousands of years in the protection against paranormal forces and for enhancement of psychic abilities.

Gemstones for Paranormal Investigations

Amber: Is said to absorb negative energy in the immediate area. Therefore, if we were to take some amber on an investigation and the atmosphere became negative, as it sometimes does, maybe the amber will be useful in dispelling some of the negative energy that persists.

Amethyst: is said to promote mental and physical clarity and is said to ward off danger. Again, this could be useful in an investigation or prior to an investigation.

After an investigation, the amethyst should be cleansed under running water.

Black Tourmaline: is a dark coloured gemstone that is said to be very effective in deflecting negativity and providing a protective shield against the paranormal and is an amazing shield against EMF. Perfect for paranormal investigation.

Celestine: Is said to be useful in contacting spirit guides. Spirit guides are guides that attach themselves to people who seek them out. A spirit guide is a being not restricted by the restraints of realms.

I have two spirit guides who currently help me communicate with spirits and I ask them to protect my group on investigations. I have a Native American Indian and an ancestor of mine who was tried during the Salem witch trials. In some investigations, my spirit guides have put me in touch with another spirit guide to help lead the investigation. I am unsure as to the reasoning of this but it is a good example of how they guide and advise their charges. They are a welcome gift on investigations. If you have not done so, try the celestine, you may be pleasantly surprised.

The Onyx: I have an onyx ring I wear. I did not know the importance of onyx when I received it however, since studying this side of paranormal investigation I began wearing it more often. Onyx is said to prevent the drain on energy often associated when channelling spirit. It is also said to protect against psychic attacks. Maybe this is why, when we did the Knowlton Church investigation the second time, although I sensed the spirit grabbing me by the throat and pushing me out of the door, I was able to stay level headed and felt no threat.

In my opinion, a serious investigator should definitely test the onyx out.

Hematite: All black gem stones can be cleansed using a powerful stone in its own right named hematite. You do this by leaving the black gemstones next to or on the hematite.

Places to Investigate

I have trailed the paranormal database and used my personal experience to list a few places that I believe to be worth investigating. Unlike other books of this nature, I have ignored local legends and myths and have only given reference to places where paranormal encounters have been recorded. If your county does not appear here, I apologise but if incidences have not been reported, I cannot give you guidance on them. I have also not listed any buildings or private premises as chances are, you will not be given permission to investigate them as a beginner, unless it is a paid event or you have your own liability insurance.

Haunted Locations of England, Bedfordshire

Flitwick manor

Sightings recorded of a white-haired woman and footsteps are heard. One report states that a white-haired woman was standing at the foot of a guest's bed, looking out of the window.

Cineworld
Screen 4 and Toilet area

Sightings of a monk/hooded figure have been recorded on a number of occasions, seen in toilet mirror and foyer.

Screen 4 is recorded as having fluctuations in temperature and staff had had stuff thrown at them, also many guests report feelings of being touched on the leg as they sat down to watch a film.

Thurleigh Airfield

Recorded is the testimony of a mod employee who was sat in the officer's mess when a door opened and shut on its own.

In another recorded incident, the witness reported the feeling of a presence in the room with him and then a light bulb shot out of the ceiling, rose and landed on the table next to him.

Footsteps through the corridors were also heard when there has been no one else in the building.

Leighton Buzzard

A stretch of road between lane and station road.

A man was driving where the two roads above meet when he saw a young dark-haired male with a long face hitchhiking.

He pulled over to offer the young male a lift and when asked where the young hitchhiker wanted to go, the hitchhiker simply pointed ahead. During the drive, the male turned to offer the young hitchhiker a cigarette and the hitchhiker was gone. The man stopped his car, looked up and down the road and looked around the area, but there was no one to be seen.

Ampthill Castle

The castle has now gone and it is now known as Ampthill Great Park. The exact location of where the castle once was is marked by a commemorative cross dedicated to Catherine of Aragon.

A knight has been seen rising from the cross. The reports are inconsistent as some say the knight has been seen wearing heavy armour while some have seen a horseman. The horseman and the knight are said to vanish at the point of the stream.

Bedford Hospital.

Over a 40-year period, there have been numerous reports from staff and patients claiming to see the figure of a beautiful girl in a long dress and coat gliding through the corridors. She has been seen passing through the walls and in the toilets.

http://www.hauntedrooms.co.uk

Haunted Locations of England, Berkshire

The Ostrich Inn, Colnbrook, Slough

Many sightings have been recorded of a Victorian lady wandering in the upstairs corridors of the inn. Also, there have been reported sightings of other ghostly figures throughout the inn.

Sport England's National Sports Centre

Formally known as Bisham Abbey

The site of many reports dating back to the First World War. All the recorded reports claim that a past tenant Mrs Hoby still haunts the grounds and is often seen rearranging rooms. It is said that she can be seen at night terrorising guests, screaming and waving her blood-soaked hands.

Newbury Market Place – Northbrook Street

There have been many recorded sightings of the ghost of an earless man walking around screaming. A grey lady has been sighted in the nearby market street and in Northbrook Street. A man has been seen dressed in black and carrying a small black bag. He vanishes suddenly.

Birch Hill, Bracknell

Red Brick Mansion, South Hill Park, Berkshire

There have been many recorded reports of various hauntings at the mansion. These include various apparitions of a child, a butler and a laundry maid. Many people have reported unexplained noises and doors opening and closing on their own.

Haunted Locations, Bristol

All Saints Church, Bristol
There have been many recorded sightings of a ghostly monk who wears black. This event has been recorded by many over the last two hundred years.

Arnos Court Graveyard, Bristol
There are many recorded sightings at this location of a woman dressed in black crying over a grave. Other reports at this location say that the ghost of a woman is seen staggering around the grave yard screaming. A common belief held regarding the screaming woman is that she had been accidently buried alive.

Coombe Dingle Bridge, Bristol
There have been several reports of a Roman soldier seen in this area.

The Old Vic Theatre, Bristol
There have been several reports of the ghost of a young woman believed to be named Sarah, seen at this location wearing a long white dress. Another report in 2010 came from a member of the staff who reported that a female voice screamed for him to get out.

Haunted locations, Buckinghamshire

High Wycombe, Cock Lane
The sighting of a woman in grey has been seen in this area heading in the direction of the old gypsy camp. One male reported that the woman began gliding down the road after him. Upon seeing the woman, the man began to run and when he could go no further, he turned around and there was nothing there.

High Wycombe, Sandage Woods
The ghost of a woman wearing lots of jewellery has been seen on the outskirts of the woods. She stands on the outskirts for several minutes before disappearing.

High Wycombe, Shopping Centre
Whilst shopping with friends, a young girl reportedly saw a transparent figure walking along the gallery above her and her friends and when she told them to look, the figure vanished.

High Wycombe, White Hill
Several people have reported hitting a man in a dark cloak whilst driving on this stretch of road but when they got out and checked for a body, there is nothing there.

West Wycombe Park Caves (The hell-fire caves)

One of the most famous hauntings is the hell-fire caves. The hell-fire caves are considered to be one of the most haunted sites in England and the caves have been investigated by hundreds of paranormal groups. There are recorded reports of a white lady, who haunts the caves, sounds of chanting and ritual are heard, as well as a lot of paranormal activity such as stones and rocks being thrown at visitors and unexplained groans are heard too.

Cambridgeshire, UK

Alconbury and Alconbury Weston, near the church
The ghost of a little drummer boy is said to follow people walking down this stretch of road at sunset playing the drums.

Bassingbourn – former RAF Bassingbourn
There have been many reports recorded of phantom air crews in this location, including sounds of an aircraft starting up. A man reported that when he lived on the site of the former airfield, he had seen the manifestation of a pair of legs dressed in uniform appear in his home.

Chesterton Road, Cambridge
One report states that whilst taking a short cut home through a car park and past an office block, the ghost of a 1940 police officer floated past them with a WWII gas mask slung over his arm.

Cambridge – Corpus Christi College
The most common haunting at this location has been reported since 1904.

It is said to be the ghost of a doctor. His ghost is seen dressed in white with long hair and a gash around his neck. Another reported that a ghost of a young woman was seen.

Cambridge – Girton College, Taylor knob staircase

Recorded hauntings have appeared to cease in this area in the 20th century. However, recorded sightings report a grey lady and previous to that, a Roman centurion.

Cheshire, UK

Bollin Hall, Cheshire, UK
Reports that Anne Boleyn has returned here after her death have been heard; however, no recorded reports have been named.

Bosley – Macclesfield Canal, first bridge Cheshire, UK
A ten-year-old girl told her mum there was a jogger and pointed to a nearby field. The mother looked and could see a black figure running towards them. But when the black figure was close enough, she could see that the black figure wore a monk's habit and under his hood, there was no face. When she turned to look at her daughter, her daughter had run back to a nearby boat and upon turning back, the monk had gone.

Boughton Heath area, Cheshire, UK
A speedy figure darts out from the side of the road crossing in front of oncoming cars but before he reaches the other side of the road, he vanishes.

Bunbury College lane, Cheshire, UK
A ghostly horse rider is said to cross the lane and vanish.

Burton Constable Hall, Cheshire, UK
A phantom nun has been recorded as standing by the secret passage. Her portraits also hang in the nun's room.

Cornwall, UK

Bodmin Jail (not a Prison anymore.)
A paranormal Investigation group who carried out an investigation at the old jail managed to evidence some EVP and reported having stones thrown at them.

Mitchell, main road through village, Cornwall
A car driver reported seeing a little girl dressed in Victorian clothes run out in front of an incoming lorry. The car driver, in shock, immediately stopped the car to get out and help but there was nothing.

Morwenstow, Tonacombe Manor, Cornwall, UK
Many apparitions and strange noises have been recorded at this site. One spirit is said to be a short balding man, another an Elizabethan woman who carries a set of keys, to name a few.

Newquay near Towan beach, Cornwall, UK
A young woman has been heard crying and seen as if she is floating near this location.

Barrow Fields, Newquay, Cornwall, UK
Home to the recorded sighting of a headless horseman, who has been seen travelling several metres above the ground in this area.

Cumbria, UK

Armathwaite Fox and Pheasant Inn, Cumbria, UK
Reports of a woman in old-fashioned clothing was reported to walk through the front door of the inn without opening the door. Also, there have been reports of the ghost of a highway man who is said to haunt this location.

Askham – area near St Peter's Church
Recorded as location that sees Lord Lonsdale pass this area by phantom coach.

Carlisle Railway Station, Cumbria, UK
Several entities are said to haunt this location, a headless man is said to haunt platform 8 and woman in a veil has been seen at this location, to name a few. The problem with investigating here besides the obvious dangers is the EMF would be overwhelming, plenty enough to provide hallucinations and sickness.

Carlisle Woodland near Heather Leigh Hall, Cumbria, UK
A former owner of the property recorded that he has seen the ghost of a man called Horace riding a black horse several times prior to the death of a loved one.

Dacre - Hawksdale hall, Cumbria, UK
On Halloween, a young lad is said to appear holding a lantern walking towards the nearby river, Caldew and when he reaches the water, he enters and vanishes.

Derby, UK

Alvaston area near the Castle, Derby, UK

Reports of the sound of battle have been recorded here on several occasions: gunfire, galloping horses and men shouting.

Pickford's House Museum, Derby, UK

There are several reported hauntings here. The first most recorded is a gardener that used to keep the grounds. It is said he can be seen working the land he used to keep. A female kitchen assistant is also a frequent haunting here and also a little girl has been seen dancing around the house.

St Mary's Bridge, Derby, UK

A phantom coach carrying a nun has been recorded here traveling over the bridge once. Upon crossing the bridge, the nun and coach vanish.

William and Glyn's Bank, Corn market, Derby UK

Three builders recorded that when they were renovating the building's basement, they knocked through to a hidden cavity, where they spotted a young boy.

When one of the builders asked him what he was doing, he said I live here and vanished.

St Helen's House, Derby, UK

There have been several recorded hauntings here.

The first is a monk that has been seen on several occasions, the second is a young girl, while the third is unknown. However, workers have recorded voices whispering their names when they are alone in the building.

Devon, UK

Berry Pomeroy Castle, Devon, UK
A possessing cavalier has been recorded as a frequent here. Also, a ghostly black dog and a child can be heard screaming and crying at this location.

Branscombe – Margell's Cottage, Devon, UK
The ghost of a man wearing a bandage around his head was recorded at this location, however other recorded hauntings are phantom monks that have been seen on a number of occasions.

Greatbid Lake manor house, Bridestow, Devon, UK
Disembodied footsteps are a common occurrence at this location. Also, the ghost of a woman has been seen on a number of occasions.

Brixham Smugglers' Haunt Hotel, Devon, UK
A shadow person could be seen sitting alone at one of the tables but only when looked at through a mirror.

Chagford – Whiddon Park guest house, Devon, UK
10th of July (reoccurring)
The last recorded sighting was in the 70s. However, annually, on the 10th of July, the spirit of a woman is seen standing in bedroom doorways, dressed in black.

Dorset, UK

Knowlton Church, Dorset, UK
One of the most active site, my team and I have investigated. We communicated with the ghosts of Neolithic people, a monk, and the ghost of a young woman and a young girl. I will not go into any more detail but please see pictures and a write up included in this book. I would consider this site one of the most active in Dorset.

West Howe Baptist Church, Dorset, UK
A woman reported that when walking home, a lady in a long white dress came from behind a tree and walked through a wall.

Banbury Rings, Dorset
My team and I investigated this site after my family and I visited the place for a day out. During the day out, my children saw a fallen log which they sat on and posed for a picture. When I got home, I uploaded the pictures and, in the background, there was what seemed to be a lady dressed in Victorian clothes to the left.

We wasted no time in investigating this site. Unfortunately, we did not communicate with the Victorian lady. However, we did record other evidence. In history, the noise of battle is also said to be heard at Banbury Rings.

Branksome Park Estate, Bournemouth, UK

At this location, it was recorded that several ghost-like children were seen playing in the grounds, dressed in brown but they were scared off.

Corfe Castle, Swanage, Dorset, UK

There are many recorded hauntings here. A shadow lady has been seen walking around the hill near the entrance. A cloaked figure has been seen in the fields around here and also the sound of galloping horses is heard. Unfortunately, this is one of the locations I contacted that have prohibited paranormal investigators from investigating the area. However, you can investigate the surrounding area.

Judge Jefferies' Restaurant, Dorchester, UK

This is one of the first places I visited unintentionally. I worked as a painter and decorator once upon a time and got a job through a friend at this location. I went outside for a cigarette and the feeling of dread and despair was overwhelming. I went back inside and spoke to my friend who was helping me decorate. Who told me about its history? There have been many recorded hauntings here as Judge Jefferies was famous for his hangings.

One of my friends and one of my sensitive investigators, John Jefferies shares the same name as the famous Judge Jefferies and could possibly be a descendent, so where possible, we use this link to draw energies.

Durham, UK

Barnard Castle, Durham, UK
Recorded sightings at this location include the reoccurring ghost of a lady being thrown into the river Tees.

Langley Park – Langley hall Ruins, Durham, UK
A headless coachman has been seen at this location but there have also been several reports spanning over a two-hundred-year period that say the building has been seen on fire and you can see soldiers running around but when investigated, the image disappears.

Weardale, the North England lead mining museum, Durham, UK
A paranormal investigation team in an attempt to raise money for charity agreed to spend the night here, but they were scared off by a ghostly woman who ran towards them screaming. Could this have been due to mass hysteria? Did someone know the location and decide to dress up and give them a fright? I would have taken this into consideration when investigating. Charity events are usually publicised in local media so someone looking to heighten the investigators' experience may have done it for a laugh.

Aycliffe – near the church, Durham, UK
A father walking with his brother and son saw a female entity wearing a Victorian dress. The figure did not have any feet and was not in contact with the ground. The entity looked at the three people before moving off.

Consett – Spring Lane, Durham, UK

The ghost of a mill worker who vanished mysteriously is seen along this lane.

Essex, UK

Coalhouse Fort, Essex, UK

This was the first paid investigation I went on with fright nights.

The sheer magnitude of the place was enough to get the imagination running overtime. The fort was set in a beautiful surrounding close to the water and in the middle of this surrounding sat a dirty old stone building protruding out of the grounds. My brother-in-law, Dave, one of the founding members of 'Everything Supernatural' and I arrived about an hour early.

We investigated the grounds and listed possible areas that may be manipulated by wind, EMF and stooges. The fort was inside a great wall and the gate would be closed throughout the investigation and there was no way to get in. After our initial recon of the site, we arrived at the front gate and asked a fort rep if this is where the ghost hunt was. The reply was, "We do not do ghost hunts. You may be in the wrong place unless of course you are here to investigate the paranormal, in which case you are in the right place."

I smiled and returned to the car for a cigarette and to tell my brother-in-law that I had just been mugged off. The sight that greeted me when returning to the car made me laugh as there were 6-10 people sharing a tub of table salt pouring it around their cars and throwing a pinch over their left shoulder. They had already lost to their imagination.

The site was extremely active and some good evidence was collected. The mediums and fright nights team were extremely professional and even when confronted by a group of lads on a stag-do who had been paid to attend the investigation. They just sat there giving the mediums grief and Fright Nights' team grief. There was plenty of contact with spirits exhibiting paranormal behaviour and loads of orbs appeared in the pictures. Loads of smells, even sulphur.

However, one of the girls who was pouring salt around her car was apparently strangled unconscious. I saw nothing strangling her, neither did the other medium and it was put down to group hysteria. As I said in the report previous to this, I had not told the medium what I could do. Only my brother-in-law knew. During the investigation, the medium/demonologist asked the group if anyone had abilities they had hid from him as two spirits wanted to make contact with them. My brother-in-law nudged me but I remained quiet at the end of the investigation. We were leaving the fort but before my brother-in-law and I left, he pulled me back.

"It was you they wanted to say hello to, right?"

I smiled at him. Dan the medium/demonologist then said that you need to train and that we can help with training, so get in touch if interested. I said I would be in touch.

Billericay – Burghstead Lodge, Essex, UK
(Now registry office and library archives, Essex, UK)

A nurse had been attending a man in this lodge for two consecutive nights when she saw that a woman stood over the man. She was recorded as wearing a green gown and a veil. The third night, the nurse saw the figure and approached her upon which, the woman removed the veil. The next day, the nurse was said to be insane and the man she was caring for was dead. A few months later, the nurse died.

Borely Church, Essex, UK

A group of paranormal investigators reported that the figure of a man stood under a tree in the church yard. Upon researching the church and its ground, the team saw a resemblance to the one-time rectory owner Harry Bull. Another recorded sighting here is that of a nun.

Boxstead – Bend Close to Boxton Road (Known as Betty Potter's Dip), Essex, UK.

On the 21st of October, annually, Betty is said to return to the spot where she was hung from a tree for witch craft. However, another theory is that she committed suicide at midnight.

Bradwell on Sea – St Peter's on the wall church. Essex, UK

Several people have reported hearing the sound of horse hooves passing by them in this area. It may be related to the recorded sighting of a Roman soldier seen on a horse at a nearby location where a Roman castle once stood.

Gloucestershire, UK

Arlingham Parish Church, Gloucestershire, UK
Several people have reported seeing a phantom old woman who has been seen in this building. She is said to give off an icy aura.

The Old Bell Hotel, Long Street, Dursley, Gloucestershire, UK
The spirit of a monk and a chambermaid has been recorded at this site. Also, a guest reported that a loud voice woke him up at 0400 hours in the morning telling him that it was 0800 hours.

Evesham, Fairford – Poulton, crossroads, Gloucestershire, UK
The shades of a coven of dark witches is said to haunt this crossroad. They were said to have plagued the town and when they died, they were buried here.

St Briavels Castle, forest of dean, Gloucestershire, UK
The castle is now a hostel and has been the site of many recorded paranormal experiences. A baby's skeleton was found behind one of the walls many years ago. The baby's cries have been heard on a number of occasions. A ghostly woman in white has also been reported and an armour-clad knight has been seen walking around. There are many

investigation groups that do paid investigations here as the place is well worth an investigation.

Fossebridge roads and surrounding areas, Gloucestershire, UK

Three men traveling in a car were followed by an old motorcycle with a side car. The rider was not wearing a helmet and the bike vanished suddenly behind them.

Hampshire, UK

Alresford - Cheriton battlefield, Hampshire, UK

On 29th March, every four years, these troops are said to be doomed to return to their former battlefield.

Bramshott Church, Hampshire, UK

A little girl wearing a bonnet has been seen here walking away from the church, disappearing through a churchyard wall.

Greenlane, Gosport, Hampshire, UK

A taxi driver had to sharply break to avoid hitting a faceless entity, which dissolved before his eyes.

Portchester – Portchester castle, Hampshire, UK

A spirit named Charlotte is the most recorded sighting here though other reports have been of a monk, who walks around outside the front of the castle, a Roman soldier and a lady who rides on the back of a white horse.

Southsea Kings' Theatre, Hampshire UK

Staff and visitors have reported seeing shadows, hearing noises investigated by Wessex ghost hunters and the team's medium recorded it as haunted. He said that it is haunted by a lady that committed suicide.

Hertfordshire, UK

Abbots Langley-churchyard and vicarage, Hertfordshire, UK

A young girl who was said to die suddenly manifests on the 31st October annually.

Ware – Presdales school woods, Hertfordshire, UK

There have been stories told for years about a hooded figure that chases people through the woods although the story has somewhat been exaggerated changing to a hooded figure with glowing eyes chasing people. There may have once been some truth to this story, definitely worth investigating.

Weston Road near Lannock Hill, Hertfordshire, UK

A woman dressed in white was seen by a husband and wife as they drove out of Weston.

Ashwell Churchyard, Hertfordshire, UK

The shadow of a headless figure is said to haunt the graveyard here.

Batford – Lower Luton road, Hertfordshire, UK

A driver had to swerve to avoid an older man who stood in the road and when they looked back, he had gone. Another report came in a couple of months later in which a similar thing was seen again, only this time by two witnesses who reported that the older man they saw had a bandage on his head and was holding an old-fashioned rifle.

Kent, UK

Biggin Hill-airport and village, Kent, UK
Reports of a phantom spitfire that has been seen and heard at the airport and in the village have been collected. There have been several reports of men in trench coats asking questions before vanishing.

Charing – Pett Lane, Kent, UK
A man driving home with his mother spotted a man wearing a mackintosh walking his dog along the lane. The car slowed down to let the man and dog cross, but they passed straight through the side of the car, lighting the car up. They then vanished with the passing.

Chilham – Woolpack Inn, Kent, UK
A grey woman has been seen here.

Dartford – A2 Road between Dartford and Bexley, Kent UK
The ghostly figure wearing black armour has been seen in this location several times.

Dover Castle, Dover, Kent, UK
An unknown soldier is the most frequently recorded sighting, a drummer boy has also been seen and in the tunnels under the castle. The place is said to be haunted by World War II soldiers and a man dressed in khaki.

Reculver – The Reculver Towers, Kent, UK

A baby has been heard crying here many times.

There have been child remains dating back to Roman times found here. They were thought to have been sacrificed to an unknown deity.

Lancashire, UK

Astley (near the canal) Lancashire, UK
A grey lady is seen in this area frequently.

Bebington Church and graveyard, Bebbington, Lancashire, UK
Robed figures are seen walking in this area but it appears they are floating due to the change in ground levels.

Bispham – Rail tracks, Lancashire, UK
A Ghostly figure is seen walking the tracks swinging his lantern.

Blackpool – Victoria Hospital, Lancashire, UK
Several staff have reported having their uniforms pulled as if a child is trying to get their attention but there is nothing there.

Goosnargh – Horns Lane, Lancashire, UK
A woman in white has been seen in the middle of the road according to several reports that reported swerving to avoid the woman, who then disappeared.

Leicestershire, UK

Braunstone Hall and Park Leicester, UK

Several phantoms are reported to haunt this area.

A young woman in white walks the corridors, a sad looking boy who looks out of the window and a phantom carriage pulled by black horses has been reported to have been seen before it vanishes into a nearby wooded area.

No further reports of interest exist at this time for Leicestershire.

Lincolnshire, UK

Lincoln, Cobb Hall

A lady in black was seen by a father minutes before she attempted to push his son down the stairs before vanishing. Luckily, the father had quick reflexes and caught his son.

No further reports of interest exist at this time for Lincolnshire.

Norfolk, UK

Burgh Castle, Norfolk, UK
Once a year, on the 27th of April, the sound of clashing swords have been heard along with raised voices, as if a battle is taking place.

Castle Rising, Norfolk, UK
Recorded reports state disembodied voices have been heard as well as laughter. Children and children signing nursery rhymes have been recorded.

Downham Market, Moat Farm, Norfolk, UK
A spooky mist has been recorded here and screaming and shouting has been heard across the fields.

Great Yarmouth, Norfolk, UK
From the 11th of July until the 14th September, a reoccurring battle between ships has been seen.

Hickling – Hickling Broad south of the village, Norfolk, UK
A female voice is heard singing and the ghost of a Napoleonic drummer boy has also been reported.

Northumberland, UK

Berwick upon Tweed churchyard, Tweedmouth, Northumberland, UK

Several locals reported seeing a phantom woman with ginger hair, dressed in white or grey. It was reported to have followed people leaving the area while others have observed a woman of the same description reading grave stones.

Haltwhistle – Bellister Castle, Northumberland, UK

The shade of a minstrel is seen about the castle.

Langley Castle, Northumberland, UK

A ghostly woman in white has been active here for some years and singing can be heard despite no one being in the castle.

Otterburn, 14th century battlefield, Northumberland, UK

A report exists that claims when a couple were visiting a site via taxi. The taxi engine died and the taxi was surrounded by phantom soldiers, who moved towards the taxi before fading away.

No further reports at this location exists at present.

Nottinghamshire, UK

Galleries of Justice, Nottinghamshire, .UK

My brother-in-law, Dave, and I did another paid investigation here with fright nights.

We started in the courtroom with a few test sensitive techniques that involved volunteers from the 20 or so investigators coming out in the front of the court room.

We were asked if anyone believed they were sensitive and if so to raise their hands. I raised my hand and was asked to come out to the front with another volunteer.

We were then told to turn our backs to the other investigators and not to look back. The other investigators were then told to all start banging their feet on the wooden floor which made a lot of noise. Two investigators were then told to come out and stand behind myself and the other volunteer. We were not allowed to look back and all the noise made it hard to pick which area they came from as we were not allowed to face them. We were then asked to describe the person standing behind us i.e. their description, personality and some questions that were asked of us. There was no doubt that the other volunteer and I were sensitives as we gave a full physical description as well as personal details only that they would know without looking at them. We then carried out the investigation guided by a medium named Ian, another great medium.

We met the ghosts of children, and prostitutes and were even asked to sit in a small cell so they could question the spirit or entity to give a full description of the order we were sat in, again not being seen by the medium or the other investigators. The three selected swapped places about five times with the cell door closed to test the abilities of the medium and it was amazingly accurate.

The spirit of a prostitute took a fancy to my brother-in-law and was able to give information on him that only my brother-in-law would know. It was a great investigation, which produced a lot of spiritual as well as scientific evidence. There was no doubt it was haunted and Ian's whose abilities were second to none, would definitely recommend this investigation.

Balderton – St Giles' Church, Nottinghamshire, UK

A grey ghost has been spotted outside the church grounds, this has been witnessed by several people.

Blyth Bridge along the A634, Nottinghamshire, UK

A ghostly woman is said to haunt this bridge and has been witnessed by several people who have felt her presence in their car when crossing the bridge.

Cuckney Church, Nottinghamshire, UK

The spirit of a woman is said to lurk around the pews and has been heard running down the right-hand side of the pews.

Elksley, A-57, Nottinghamshire, UK

A bus driver and a conductor reported that they hit a dark shadow that screamed. Before impact, they bought the bus to a halt and searched the area but there was nothing there.

Oxfordshire, UK

In 2015, I worked in Immigration transport for a while. It was in Oxfordshire, that despite my experience in the paranormal, I witnessed probably the most surreal paranormal experience I had ever seen.

I was on duty with my colleague and friend Tracy. Tracy is also very sensitive but the night I speak of, we were talking about the job in hand. We were tasked to pick three people up from a prison in Wales and take them to Campsfield House in Oxfordshire. We picked up the detainees as usual and made our way to Campsfield House. I forgot what the motorway we were traveling on in Oxfordshire was named but it was surrounded by fields and there were no houses in the area for at least 50 miles.

Tracy was driving and I was checking on the detainees in the back of the van when all of a sudden, we saw something in front of the van. We were travelling at about 50 miles per hour. All of a sudden, in front of the van stood a young male dressed in a 90s tracksuit struggling with friends in the road. The tracksuit was grey shell suit type material. Tracy slammed on the breaks and the front of the van lit up and we could see that the male was play fighting with friends in the middle of the road.

As we made impact, there was no noise, but we stopped the van when it was safe to do so looking back down the road. We could see nothing. Then we checked the van for damage and there was nothing. We phoned the police to let them know what happened and they said to continue to the destination. We spoke to the detainees who were also shook up. They said, "Don't worry, at least you didn't hit anything."

We saw him but he was being pulled by something. We couldn't see any faces but only shadows pulling the man's arms backwards. They then vanished and left us shaken up. We continued the journey to Campsfield House where we dropped the detainees off and as they left with the officers, they patted us on the backs, "Don't worry, you didn't hit him; he wasn't there."

The police phoned us back and they found nothing despite closing the road and doing a detailed search of the surrounding fields and the road, no debris, no blood and no clothing. Tracy and I sat for about an hour talking about what we had just witnessed. I still have no explanation and neither does Tracy. We researched the area to see if there had been any similar reports and unfortunately, there were none but there was a report of a coach crash in the same area that crashed during a school trip in the late 80s.

Chipping Norton, Church and surrounding area, Oxfordshire, UK

A holy man is seen walking around the church and the grounds.

East Haney, road close to the bridge, Oxfordshire, UK

A man wearing an overcoat and a hat jumps in front of cars and vanishes upon impact.

Hempton, main road through village, Oxfordshire, UK

Several people have recorded being physically pushed off their bicycles in this area.

Milton Common – Church of St Michael and all angels, Oxfordshire, UK

Dressed in Tudor clothing, the grey lady has been observed moving across the churchyard.

Shropshire, UK

Acton Burnell Castle, Shropshire, UK
A ghostly girl in white has been seen in the grounds of the castle and in 2004, a girl on a school trip managed to capture a photograph of a misty face.

Astley Abbot – main road through village, Shropshire, UK
A ghost woman in a long, white dress has been seen along the road here by motorists before vanishing.

Brosley – ruined churchyard, Shropshire, UK
A spirit was witnessed walking through the grave yard wearing a bonnet and carrying a candle. She quickly disappeared when seen.

Ironbridge Power Station, Shropshire, UK
Several workers at the power station reported seeing a ghostly monk and in the grounds. A witness reported seeing a woman float into his path before vanishing.

Chatwell – general area, Shropshire, UK
A ghostly figure on horseback has been reported riding around the lanes leading to the nearby village.

Somerset, UK

Strogumber, Heddon Oak tree, Somerset, UK

The shades of many soldiers are seen hanging from this tree and have been reported around the surrounding area.

Taunton A38 road near the town

A man in a dark cloak has been seen standing by the roadside and if the driver that sees him does not stop for him, he throws himself in front of the car before vanishing.

No further reports.

Staffordshire, UK

Alton Towers

Many myths and reports surround Alton towers recently, following the serious accident that led to many people having life-changing injuries physically and mentally.

People are cashing in on this event by claiming to catch many pictures of spirits and ghosts that they claim were responsible for the accident. In my opinion, this event was due to negligence and nothing more and making money out of people's tragedy is something I will not partake in. There are many spirits etc. that have been recorded here for hundreds of years and the most haunted teams have also investigated the site. The recent reports seem to be a result of mass hysteria and nothing more so in my opinion. This is definitely a site not to be dismissed for its activity, but I hope people start investigating the area as investigators and not people jumping on the proverbial bandwagon, trying to make a quick buck from people's tragedy.

No further reports exist.

Suffolk, UK

Junction 12, A12, between Jay Lane and Rackham's corner, Suffolk, UK.
There have been many reports on this stretch of roads of phantom jay walkers and a phantom cyclist. Many have reported hitting the jaywalker and cyclist feeling a bump but when they stop to investigate, it disappears. None of them have ever existed.

Beck Row – Aspel Farm, found along the road from Beck Row to Holly Well Road, Suffolk, UK
Here there was a recorded sighting of a large entity that appeared in front of a group of locals. He said do not fear me but fear what follows me, he then vanished. When he vanished, they reported a large gust of wind went past them.

No further reports exist.

Surrey, UK

Bletchington Church, Surrey, UK
A woman wearing a seventeenth century dress has been seen wandering the graveyard.

Bramley – Chinhurst Woods, Surrey, UK
A crossroads near the woods is haunted by an old traveller woman and an old horse that have been seen here.

Caterham – Area around the A22, Surrey, UK
Several motorists have claimed to see eight dark figures dressed in black cloaks, running around, heading towards the duel carriageway. They were reportedly moving in silence.

Guildford Castle, Surrey, UK
A woman in Victorian clothing has been seen walking around the grounds.

Horsell Woods – path leading to pond, Surrey, UK
A ghostly figure floated past one witness. Its legs could not be seen, only its knees.

No further reports.

Warwickshire, UK

Alcester – A435, Warwickshire, UK

There have been many recorded sightings of a middle-aged lady in a beige rain coat along this road, sometimes walking, sometimes pushing a bike. One motorist reported hitting her before she vanished without a trace. He panicked and reported it to the local police who said many motorists had reported the same incidence.

Alveston – Mill Lane, Warwickshire, UK

A father and son were camping close to the river Avon, when they heard singing or chanting outside of their tent and when they got the courage up to open their tent, there was nothing there and the singing stopped.

No further reports.

There are many texts and online references to reoccurring hauntings. These are said to follow various patterns of reoccurrence.

This type of haunting is reportedly residual. Personally, my team and I do not bother with this type of haunting as if you can find it online so can millions of other people. So therefore, people may doctor this occurrence for custom or publicity. However, I will list below some of the most popular reoccurring hauntings that have been recorded and you can make your own mind up as whether to investigate this type of haunting or not.

January the 19th

Braddock down, Cornwall, UK

It is said that on this day the sound of horse hooves echo throughout.

Historical Info: This is recorded as the site where Cromwell's army was defeated in the year 1643 during the English civil war.

February

Tower of London

12th: A white shape is said to appear in the bloody tower in the tower of London.

Goodwin Sands, Kent, UK

13th: Every 50 years, the three-mast ship, the Lady Luvibond, is seen to sail from the location it sunk in 1748.

Reoccurring residual hauntings continued.

February

Hickling Broad, Norfolk, UK

15th: A drummer boy is recorded to be seen.

March

The Ferry Boat Inn, Cambridgeshire, UK

A suicide victim appears annually.

April

Rochester Castle, Kent, UK
4th: Lady Blanche de Warren is seen.

Orme House, Isle of white, UK
9th: An eighteenth century lady is seen walking around.

May

Blickling Hall, Norfolk, UK
19th: A phantom coach is seen heading towards Blickling Hall.

Potter Heigham, Norfolk, UK
31st: A coach crashes into an old bridge at Potter Heigham.

July

Somerset, UK
5th: Soldiers have been seen, horse hooves heard and sounds of a battle are heard in the Marsh Lands, where battle of Sedgemoor was fought in 1685.

Reoccurring residual hauntings continued.

August

Chicksands Priory, Bedfordshire, UK
17th: The ghost of a nun is seen at the location.

September

Sherborne Castle, England
28th: Sir Walter Raleigh is seen at the location.

The Grenadier Inn, Hyde Park corner, London, UK
A **19th** century grenadier guard who was murdered is seen at the inn this month.

October

Warwickshire, the site of the battle of Edgehill in 1642
23rd: Battle sounds are heard and soldiers are seen.

November

Hyde Hall, Hertfordshire, UK
1st: A horseman is seen on his white horse.

Bruce Castle, north London
3rd: Costania, Lady Coleraine, returns to the site where she took her life.

December

Stiper Stones, Shropshire, UK
21st: All spirits of Britain are said to meet at the above location for the longest night of the year.

Samhain, October 31st
Samhain is a Celtic/pagan holiday where the veil between the earth realm and spirit realm is its thinnest. Another holiday

that was hijacked by Christianity to devalue its true origins. It is now named Halloween or All Saints Day.

On this date, pagan and Celtic people gather to celebrate the ancestors that came before them and if they are fortunate enough they will be able to communicate with them. This is my favourite holiday, although very commercial now, but knowing its true origins, I enjoy this holiday the most. It is a celebration of the dead and their time with us. Whatever your religion or belief, nearly everyone now celebrates the holiday.

My Samhain involves me dressing up with my children. I currently live on a council estate which has about 80 houses on it. Every child on the estate then gathers with their parents and wanders around the estate, collecting sweets. My partner takes my children and I stay behind to hand out sweets and in between answering the door to the children, I begin to prepare myself for a busy night ahead.

The true pagan holiday lasts three days. In between answering the doors to children and handing out sweets, I get my normal tarot cards out, my Celtic tarot cards and open myself up to channel. Once the trick or treating is over, I put my children to bed, say goodnight to my partner who also goes to bed and my night begins. I used to set up the laptop when the most haunted life was on and watch all of the cameras, stopping only to communicate with any spirits that came to me. I now read my tarots to answer specific questions as I find this also helps with channelling.

As a paranormal investigator, if I did not have children, I would definitely be out investigating. If you have no children and no other commitments, I advise you to get yourself out investigating on the 31st October and celebrate your ancestors, maybe even have a sanctioned séance, but only if you are with someone experienced in the paranormal, as the veil between realms is thinner and you may be lucky to communicate with a passed family member. However, if you are not with someone experienced, you may end up inviting something or someone else in and that is not as welcome.

Séance vs. Ouija Board

A séance does not have to involve a Ouija board and I do not condone the use of Ouija boards. This may be because every time I had a heart to heart with my mum, she told me: "If you use a Ouija board, I will know."

She would then tell me the story of how she had used a Ouija board with friends when I was little. She made sure I was staying with my nan. She and her two friends, my Aunt Jan and Aunty Corrine, sat down to do the Ouija board. My mum, although aware of her heritage, knew that her gifts were untrained. I cannot remember the full story now but whatever it was that they had made contact with, had attached itself to my mum, probably due to her gifts being untrained. I do not know if she ever told me the full extent of this attachment but I do remember it ended up with my mum having to seek out a medium to remove the entity.

Therefore, for this reason, I have never used a Ouija board and have no intention of ever using one in the future. A séance however, is equally as effective and much safer. Below, I will give you a rough guide to conducting a séance.

Conducting a Séance

This will appear to more spiritual in nature than investigative, but a séance can help produce more solid evidence.

Items you will need

Candles
Red light
Pictures of all at the séance (optional)
A table
A glass (optional)
A pendulum (optional)

The first rule of a séance is that everyone that sits in on the séance needs to believe or have a healthy interest in the paranormal. This is not saying that sceptics are not welcome to observe the séance but they cannot sit around the table it is conducted from.

Preparation

The candles are lit and placed in the centre of the table.

If you have pictures, spread these out around the table and do not have your own picture in front of you, mix them up with the others at the séance.

The red light is placed in front of the séance leader, preferably a medium or a sensitive or the person with the most experience.

The idea of this is that if anything unwanted comes through, it will focus on the medium or sensitive or experienced member and not seek out the weak or scared.

Beginning the séance, everyone involved must join hands and a blessing must be performed before going any further.

You can say something like.

"As we conduct this séance, we invite all who come in love to communicate with us with no malice or false intentions"

*If you know who your spirit guide is, name them at this point and ask them to watch over you during the séance.

But you can ask for protection from whatever you believe in. You could also do the visual exercise we spoke about earlier. It is your choice but make sure you do it to be safe.

Depending on what you decide to use, a pendulum, a glass and pictures or table rapping, a séance can provide great evidence of the paranormal.

Glass and Picture Method

If you use the pictures and glass method, ask everyone involved in the séance to place a finger on the glass. When this is achieved, ask the spirit to choose who their message is for or who they would like to speak to by sliding the glass to the picture of the person.

The medium, sensitive or experienced member will decide if the chosen member will be safe to take the message or ask that the spirit communicates with them only. Many séances will tell you not to take anything electrical into the séance and I agree to an extent due to the EMF given off of manmade objects. But, if someone wanted to record the séance on a Dictaphone or a camcorder, this would be beneficial to the investigation.

The Pendulum Method

I would use a crystal pendulum when carrying out this kind of séance, but I have seen some people use very good wooden ones made from natural woods. You ask the spirit to turn the pendulum clockwise for yes and anti-clockwise for no when questions are asked.

My problem with pendulum séances is that many factors can affect a pendulum; after all it is a weighted object with a string through it. So wind, breath, hand tremors can all influence a pendulum to move. However, my mum used my partner's necklace to predict the sex of my children to good effect.

Table Rapping

Table rapping is the method used most by my group and I. In this, if everyone is holding hands, no one bangs the table, tainting the investigation. In this method, everyone joins hands around the table.

We use the calling out method we discussed earlier to illicit a response from the spirit/ghost/entity, which is usually one tap for yes and two taps for no. We may even place a bell away from the table or a flashing touch toy to be sure no one is influencing the investigation. Then, we ask the spirit ghost entity to ring the bell or touch the flash toy.

This can also be done using a pressure pad, which can be bought or made but either way, they are quite expensive. But it is worth checking out Viper Paranormal on YouTube. By the time this book comes out, there may be a video on how to make one cheaper.

Courses

There are many courses that can enhance your paranormal investigations and one of the recent ones I have found is an exorcism course that you can do online. It is taught by Bob Larson, a man famous in his own right in Arizona for Christian exorcisms. He has written many books on the subject and is now offering online courses.

Course

http://internationalschoolofexorcism.org/course-levels/

One of the courses I recommend highly is the psychic retreats offered by Fright Nights, which teaches you the basic skills and then throws you into an investigation that you lead. I like this method as I learn better being thrown in at the deep end and I genuinely learnt to swim this way so this method suits me.

However, if you google mediumship courses, thousands come up with many to list in this book.

Some of the courses I suggest you look for are:

Demonology courses
Mediumship courses
Spiritualism courses

There are also many YouTube videos that can provide training in the above areas but again, it is up to you.

Other Groups and Organisations

The best resource for other groups and organisations in the UK and Ireland can be found on the link below.

I do not personally know any of the groups below but I do use the paranormal database to find locations.

http://www.paranormaldatabase.com/forms/submissiont hanks.htm

- *www.ghost-mysteries.com* – providing first-hand accounts, images, information and discussion into the paranormal world.
- *www.hayleyisaghost.co.UK* – the blog of Hayley Stevens, former believer turned sceptical activist, and writer of some pretty honest words.
- *www.strangenorth-eastderbyshire.UK* – This site aims to catalogue all the known strange phenomena and traditions of Chesterfield, Bolsover and North-East Derbyshire that have occurred down the years and forms one part of ASSAP's Project Albion.
- http://www.paranormap.net – Like the Paranormal Database, only based in Greece and in Greek!
- *http://ghostsofredditch.weebly.com* – 'From legless monks, ghostly horses and old secret tunnels, Redditch seems to have a lot more to it than meets the eye!'
- *www.paraspear.com* – A place to read and share paranormal experiences, to explore research on

parapsychological phenomena and to continue the debate that surrounds the study of Psi.

- *https://freakyfolktales.wordpress.com* – Freaky Folk Tales (a haunting we will go…) documents legends and hauntings across southern Britain.
- *http://newsfromthespiritworld.com* – Reporting on weird and strange news from around the world.
- *http://alien-ufo-research.com* – UFO news and case studies from the world over.
- *www.ghostlyvoices.net* – An overview of 'this fascinating and all-important branch of paranormal research'.
- *www.cornwall-ufo.co.UK* – the Cornwall UFO Research Group (CUFORG) was formed in October 1995, following an experience of founding member Dave Gillham.
- *www.theparanormal.ca/index.html* – a roundup of news, talk, lists films and special features from the world of the paranormal.
- *http://psychicrevolution.com* – sharing paranormal experiences, both via an anonymous paranormal phenomena survey and on the website.
- *www.legendsofkent.co.UK* – Fascinating myths, legends, ghosts and mysteries from Kent, ordered chronologically for ease of use.
- *www.rosegarnett.com* – short stories of the supernatural, set in Edinburgh.
- *http://paranthropology.weebly.com* – Jack Hunter's transpersonal anthropology website, taking a subjective look at the paranormal.
- *www.andrewcollins.com* – Author Andrew Collin's website, featuring many great articles on the Cygnus mystery, angels, earth mysteries and details of Andrew's works and appearances.
- *http://eppingforestghosts.webs.com* – working towards a definitive collection of ghost stories about Epping Forest and the areas around it.

- *http://www.aformerskeptic.com* – a former sceptic's view of ghosts, hauntings and the paranormal.
- *www.ghostsstory.com* – a collection of true ghost stories and paranormal photographs.
- www.evp-voices.com – Dutch site dealing with Electronic Voice Phenomena.
- *http://gothic-portal.awardspace.com* – dark life of the gothic subculture, gothic fashion, gothic poems and goths culture.
- *www.ghosthuntingaustralia.blogspot.com* – a site mainly dedicated to Australian folklore, whether old or not yet discovered.
- *www.paradoxelectronics.com* – a paranormal investigator who designs and builds his own equipment.
- *www.mysterial.co.UK* – a free facility for the community of people and organisations with shared interests in the unexplained
- *http://www.anomalousexperience.com* – set up to share real anomalous experiences and read about the experiences of others.
- *www.yourparanormal.co.UK* – online community of ghosts, monsters, UFO's, the occult and the otherwise unexplained.
- www.sceptictel.co.UK – views of a sceptic believer...
- *www.ufoencounters.co.UK* – UFOEncounters.co.UK was formed in late 2005 to offer a unique reference point on UFO sightings, facts and myths.
- *www.studiesoftheparanormal.com* – a selection of essays concerning the paranormal
- *www.yourghoststories.com* – a site for publishing, sharing and reading real ghosts stories from real people
- *www.ghost-story.co.UK* – First-hand ghost stories and other paranormal accounts, covering the UK and beyond.

- *www.spookystuff.co.UK* – formed in late 2005 to offer a unique reference point on everything about the paranormal.
- *www.sightingseekers.com* – Ghosts stories, pictures, videos, EVP, and haunting community
- *www.harryprice.co.UK* – dedicated to the life and work of pioneering psychical researcher and ghost-hunter Harry Price.
- *www.ghostisland.com* – ghostly reports and stories from the Isle of Wight.
- *www.paranormality.com* – 'The A to Z of paranormal, supernatural, weird and unusual phenomena.'
- *www.ghosts.org* – a huge collection of paranormal links.
- *www.mysteriousbritain.co.UK* – a roundup of stories and legends from across the UK.
- *www.forteantimes.com* – online version of the classic magazine.
- *www.paranormalnews.com* – a roundup of paranormal news, spanning the globe.
- *www.nipra.co.UK* – Irish ghost stories
- *www.trueghoststories.co.UK* – Real life ghost stories and hauntings from around the world.
- *www.conspiracycity.com* – Conspiracies, cryptozoology, and a very large number of paranormal links.
- *www.hauntedhovel.com* – dedicated to providing the reader with as much information about ghosts and everything related to them.
- *www.ghostsandstories.com* – A home for ghosts and ghost stories.
- *www.freewebs.com/faeden* – The UK Paranormal Tavern covers all aspects of the paranormal and supernatural.

- *www.everythingaberystwyth.co.UK/ghosts-of-aberystwyth* – a large collection of Aberystwyth ghosts and local hauntings.
- *www.syfy.co.UK* – As well as covering a wealth of old and new SF and paranormal shows and news, the site has a growing paranormal community.
- *http://penrhynghosts.blogspot.com* – Blogger researching and documenting the ghosts of Penrhyn Castle, Bangor.
- *https://themosthauntedtowninengland.wordpress.com* – A blog following paranormal activities in Lethmachen, England.
- *http://everythingghost.co.UK* – a group of friends who share an interest in all things ghost, from a love of hearing traditional ghost stories, to conducting serious investigations into supposed haunted locations.

UK and Ireland:

- *www.ghostclub.org.UK* – founded in 1862, The Ghost Club is the oldest organisation in the world associated with psychical research.
- *www.gghUK.co.UK* – Gloucester Ghost Hunters is a group from Gloucester UK made up of enthusiasts within the field of the paranormal.
- *http://nspr.weebly.com* – Nottingham Scientific Paranormal Research is a team of enthusiasts who investigate reports of paranormal activity, providing a free, discrete, confidential service in homes and workplaces.
- *www.leicester-ghost-hunters.co.UK* – a small team based in the heart of Leicester, aiming to gather as much evidence of the paranormal as possible.
- *www.7paranormal.org* – A paranormal team formed 2010 and based in Sunderland.

- *http://twilightparanormal.co.UK* – a team of honest and like-minded investigators, sensitives and mediums, aiming to offer an honest account of the paranormal.
- *www.irishghosthunters.com* – an Ireland-based team of paranormal investigators founded by Irish national radio Today FM DJ Tim Kelly
- *www.infinityparanormal.co.UK* – a paranormal group comprised of dedicated paranormal investigators with many years of experience at private residences, commercial and historic locations.
- *www.ppurs.webeden.co.UK* – formed in 2010 and are dedicated and committed to investigating, documenting and sometimes removal of paranormal phenomena across South Wales.
- *www.ghost-science.co.UK* – a small team dedicated to scientific paranormal research in the Milton Keynes area.
- *www.phxi.co.UK* – Established in 1996 for the investigation, detection and removal of paranormal phenomena in the UK.
- *www.the-spi.co.UK* – Sussex Paranormal Investigators has been formed to study and investigate paranormal activity, with the sole aim to give a balanced view on evidence gathered and to present this to the public domain.
- *http://midlothianparanormalinvestigations.synthasit e.com* – formed in 2008, Midlothian Paranormal Investigations are a non-profit group using various equipment in their investigations.
- *http://praofi.org* – an Irish Paranormal Research Group dedicated to researching all things Paranormal through exclusively scientific means.
- *http://teamspiritz.webs.com* – Team Spiritz are a non-profit paranormal investigation team based in the Dudley area of the West Midlands.

- *www.supernaturalinvestigations.org.UK* — an experienced team of serious paranormal researchers comprised of those with both scientific and psychic approaches.
- *www.spiritteamUK.com* – a group of professionally trained individuals, set up in 2004 to investigate and promote research into the paranormal.
- *www.spookythings.iofw.co.UK* – All the latest spooky stories, and ghostly encounters from the world's most haunted island.
- *www.moonslipper.com* – a small group that investigates and solves paranormal situations, based in Co. Wexford, Ireland.
- *www.avonparanormalteam.co.UK* – a newly formed paranormal group from Bristol who like to investigate alleged hauntings anywhere within the UK.
- *www.birminghamghosts.webeden.co.UK* – dedicated to Birmingham and the surrounding areas, investigating free of charge for the importance of paranormal research.
- *www.ghostfinder.co.UK* – Ghostfinder Paranormal Society is a investigation team that was set up with the intention of helping more people understand and find answers to the paranormal.
- *www.shadowseekers.co.UK* – a non-profit making group based in the North-West region of the UK organising overnight investigations in our quest to find evidence of the paranormal.
- *www.northantshaunted.co.UK* – an established group of individuals interested in the paranormal and haunted locations around Northamptonshire.
- *http://bpitparanormal.webs.com* – established in November 2011, BPIT use a variety of tools to seek out aspects of the paranormal.
- *www.leinsterparanormal.com* – an Ireland (Carlow)-based group of people with an interest in the phenomena commonly referred to as 'ghosts'.

- *www.ghostconnections.com* – Investigations carried out in a professional manner by a small core team all over the UK.
- *www.freewebs.com/hauntedyorkshire* – Specialising in private houses, and other haunted locations. All investigations are free of charge.
- *www.hampshireghostclub.net* – a large, diverse website and forum dealing with hauntings and ghost hunting
- *www.swpr.co.UK* – Home of the South Wales Paranormal Team, investigating reports of apparitions, hauntings and other spontaneous paranormal phenomena.
- *www.lutonparanormal.com* – The Luton Paranormal Society web page, covering the Bedfordshire region.
- *www.ghostquest.freeserve.co.UK* – a northern ghost investigation unit.
- *www.nepsUK.org* – based in northeast England, NEPS is a group of family and friends set on the investigation and research of paranormal phenomenon.
- *www.midlandparanormal.co.UK* – Midland Paranormal Investigations are a group which take the study of ghosts and hauntings seriously, covering the whole of the Midlands.
- *www.parasearch.org.UK* – West Midlands group which investigates the paranormal in a scientific and objective manner whilst maintaining the view that human beings have a transcendent essence that may reveal other realms of reality.
- *www.upia.co.UK* – The Unknown Phenomena Investigation Association (UPIA) was formed in 1998 to actively research and investigate the majority of paranormal events.
- *www.northern-ghost-investigations.com* – The Northern Ghost Investigations Team are a group of investigators from Teesside and Sunderland areas.

- *www.itsbehindyou.co.UK* – a Telford-based group researching the paranormal and anything to do with ghosts.
- *www.project-reveal.moonfruit.com* – Ghost hunting group based in Rotherham.
- *http://dorsetghostinvestigators.tv/* – Two ordinary men that have set out to discover whether ghosts and spirits exist, searching all over the UK.
- *http://nlpi.co.UK* – North London Paranormal Investigations was created from a like-minded group of professional individuals who go about their normal lives from day to day but who also shared a common interest – the paranormal.
- *http://findthetruth.jimdo.com/* – An organisation seeking to locate and document apparent paranormal phenomenon through the application of historical research, scientific methodology and a knowledge of ancient spiritual beliefs.
- *http://www.rsvpUK.org.UK/ - RSVP UK* are a team of experienced professionals who research and investigate the paranormal for free, having formed in 2012 after many years doing paranormal events.
- *http://lanarkshireparanormal.co.UK* – Lanarkshire Paranormal are a dedicated team of paranormal researchers based in Scotland.
- *www.paranormalunited.co.UK* – Paranormal United, based in Bridgnorth Shropshire are a team of paranormal enthusiasts and ghost hunters who have a simple mission statement. To provide the information needed for likeminded people to explore the paranormal and decide, with an open mind whether they believe.
- *http://oxfordshireandberkshireparanormal.co.UK* – A non-profit group based in Oxfordshire and Berkshire, with a team made up of believers, sceptics, sceptical believers, mediums and sensitives.

- *www.clubzeroparanormal.co.UK* – Based in Stockport, just outside Manchester in the United Kingdom, ClubZero and its team adhere to a professional approach, using rational and scientific methods.

Thank You

Thank you to the paranormal database for allowing me to use your site as a resource. http://paranormaldatabase.com

Thank you to all that laughed when I said I was writing a book as you fuelled me to complete it.

Thank you to my spirit guides who continue to guide me and protect my group and I. I also thank my ancestry, which has provided me with a gift.

Thank you to my group, 'Everything Supernatural' for sticking by me and continuing to help me find and research new theories on paranormal investigation. I could not do it without you.

Ending

If you would like to join us on an investigation, please contact everythingsupernatural8@gmail.com.

Please contact us if you have somewhere you would like us to investigate.

Stay Blessed.
Stay safe out there and keep investigating.